W9-BUK-204

HOW? WHO? WHAT? WHEN? WHERE? WHY?

Questions
kids
ask

INDEX

PUBLISHER	Joseph R. DeVarennes	
PUBLICATION DIRECTOR	Kenneth H. Pearson	
ADVISORS	Roger Aubin	
	Robert Furlonger	
EDITORIAL SUPERVISOR	Jocelyn Smyth	
PRODUCTION MANAGER	Ernest Homewood	
PRODUCTION ASSISTANTS	Martine Gingras	Kathy Kishimoto
	Catherine Gordon	Peter Thomlison
CONTRIBUTORS	Alison Dickie	Nancy Prasad
	Bill Ivy	Lois Rock
	Jacqueline Kendel	Merebeth Switzer
	Anne Langdon	Dave Taylor
	Sheila Macdonald	Alison Tharen
	Susan Marshall	Donna Thomson
	Pamela Martin	Pam Young
	Colin McCance	
SENIOR EDITOR	Robin Rivers	
EDITORS	Brian Cross	Ann Martin
	Anne Louise Mahoney	Mayta Tannenbaum
PUBLICATION ADMINISTRATOR	Anna Good	
ART AND DESIGN	Richard Comely	Ronald Migliore
	Robert B. Curry	Penelope Moir
	George Elliott	Marion Stuck
	Marilyn James	Bill Suddick
	Robert Johanssen	Sue Wilkinson

Canadian Cataloguing in Publication Data

Main entry under title:

Questions kids ask : index

Supplement to the series Questions kids ask.
ISBN 0-7172-2567-4

1. Questions kids ask—Indexes.
2. Children's questions and answers—Indexes.
I. Smyth, Jocelyn.   II. Comely, Richard.   III. Series.

AG195.Q485 1988   j031'.02   C89-093177-1

Copyright © 1989 by Grolier Limited. All rights reserved.
Printed and Bound in U.S.A.

This index is an alphabetical listing of information found in the 27 volumes of *Questions Kids Ask*.

The first number following each entry refers to the volume and the second number indicates the page. For example, ''abacus, 18-22'' shows that the abacus entry is in volume 18 on page 22.

Numbers in **bold type** show where a definition for an entry can be found.

A

abacus, 18-22
Abominable Snowman, 16-28
Achilles, 16-18, 25-24
''Achilles' heel,'' 25-24
Achilles tendon, 25-25
acid rain, 20-28
acrobatics, 10-29
acronym, **25-17**
adrenalin, **19-11**
Adventures of Pinocchio, The, 26-9
aerosol, **22-24**
aerosol can, 22-24
aesthetic, **10-5**
aging, 2-22
air, 3-10, 3-11, 3-17, **20-10**, 23-22
air conditioner, 22-26
air pressure, **15-30**, 20-10, 20-11
    and lift, 22-14
air resistance, 18-21
airplane, 18-31, 22-14
Aladdin, 26-7
alarm clock, 13-23

albatross, 7-17, 7-20
albino, 19-12
Aldrin, Edwin Jr., 6-30
algae, 9-5, 9-11, 9-14, 9-15
Ali Baba, 26-7
Alice's Adventures in Wonderland, 26-14
''all the tea in China,'' 25-30
allergy, 18-24, 19-22
alligator, 17-18
alloy, **18-28**
Amazon, 24-24
ambrosia, **27-21**
America, name of, 21-15
America's Cup, 4-14
amphibian, **17-5**
anaconda, 17-14
anagram, 25-29
Andes, 24-29
anenometer, 20-26
Angel Falls, 3-23
angler, **4-30**

angler fish, 5-29
ant, 1-14, 1-22, 1-23, 11-22, 11-23, 11-25
Antarctic, 3-25
Antarctica, 3-9, 3-30, 6-27, 20-12, 20-13
antelope, 14-19, 14-31
antenna
    insect, 1-14, 1-23, 11-22
    radio, television and radar, 22-7
antipodes, 25-29
antler, 14-19
ape, 14-9
    blinking, 2-21
Aphrodite, 16-16
apple, 25-15
Appleseed, Johnny, 6-24
appleworm, 11-18
April Fool's Day, 8-10
arachnids, 11-7. *See also* spider
Archimedes, 18-28

Arctic, 20-12
Arctic Circle, 3-9, 3-25
Arctic tern, 7-14
armor, 21-7
Armstrong, Neil, 6-30
army ant, 11-22
art restoration, 10-6
Artemis, 4-29
asteroid, 3-16
astronomer, **3-12**
Athena, 16-11, 16-12
Atlantis, 16-22
Atlas, 16-19, 25-10
atmosphere, **20-11**
atom, **18-19**
Attila the Hun, 27-23
aubergine, 9-6
aurora borealis, 23-19
auxin, 9-11
avalanche, 3-15
Aztecs, 21-16

B

backbone, 19-30
bacteria, 12-15, 12-24, 12-25, 13-7, 18-24
bad luck. *See* luck
baked Alaska, 12-26
bald eagle, 1-12
baldness, 19-24
ball
    largest, 4-25

    rubber, 4-22
ballet, 10-8
balloon
    helium, 3-10
    hot air, 13-10
    toy, 13-10
bamboo, 9-27
banana, 9-6, 12-16
Band-Aids, 13-8

bank swallow, 7-27
bark, 9-20
barnacle, 5-10
barometer, 20-10, 20-11
barracuda, 5-6
Barrie, James, 26-8
baseball, 4-9
basketball, 4-9
bat, 14-6, 14-7
bathtub, 15-6
baton, conductor's, 10-15
battery, 22-30
Battle of Waterloo, 23-21
Bay of Fundy, 3-25
bear, 14-7
beating, 4-15
Beatles, The, 6-29
beaver, 14-16, 14-17
bee, 1-22, 1-23, 5-6, 11-8, 11-9, 11-28,
    11-29
"bee in your bonnet," 25-23
beet, sugar, 12-27
Beethoven, Ludwig von, 10-26
beetle, 11-10, 11-11
belladonna, 9-29
Bellerophon, 16-11
belly button, 2-5
Berlin Wall, 21-31
Bermuda Triangle, 24-5
Berserkers, 16-20
"between the devil and the deep blue
    sea," 25-12
bicycle, 4-18, 4-19
    fastest, 13-18
    invention of, 13-18
Big Ben, 24-26
Big Dipper, 3-12

Bigfoot, 16-28
binary code, 18-23
bird
    bathing, 7-19
    beak, 7-13
    calls, 7-10
    communication, 1-14
    egg, 7-22, 7-23
    egg tooth, 7-22
    feet, 7-6, 7-7
    flight, 1-19, 7-20, 7-21
    hatching, 7-22
    hearing, 7-11
    mating, 1-12, 7-25
    migration, 1-18
    nest, 7-8, 7-9, 7-26, 7-27
    perching, 7-6
    sleeping, 7-6
    smallest, 1-26
    song, 7-10
    types of, 7-5
    wings, 7-20
    young, 7-24
bird's nest soup, 12-31
Black Death, 21-18
black seadevil, 5-26
black widow spider, 11-7
bladderwort, 17-27
Blarney Stone, 8-22
blimp, 18-20
blindworm, 17-12
blinking, 2-21
blood, human, 2-24, 19-7, 19-8, 19-16,
    19-17
    circulation, 19-10
blue, 18-17
blue jay, 7-24

blue jeans, 13-26
blue whale, 1-24, 1-25, 14-5
blushing, 2-24
boat
    ice, 4-15
    sail, 4-14, 4-15
bogeyman, 26-13
Boleyn, Anne, 6-8
bone, human, 2-9, 19-7
    biggest, 2-8
    number of, 19-21
    smallest, 2-8
Bonnie Prince Charlie, 6-9
boomerang, 4-23
Borglum, Gutzon, 6-30
botanist, 9-30
Botany Bay, 9-30
botfly, 11-15
bower bird, 7-9
bowling, 27-9
Boxing Day, 8-13
Boyoma Falls, 3-23
Braille, Louis, 13-15
braille, 13-15
brain, human, 2-16, 2-20, 2-28, 2-29,
    2-31, 19-27

aging of, 2-22
bread slicing machine, 22-27
breakfast cereal, 27-6
breathing
    amphibian, 17-8
    fish, 5-22
    human, 19-16
    lizard, 17-29
    plant, 9-25
    turtle, 17-10
Bridge of Sighs, 24-18
Brobdingnag, 26-20
bruise, 19-7
bubonic plague, 21-18
buccaneers, 21-29
buffalo, 21-8
Buffalo Bill, 6-10, 6-11
bull's eye, 4-31
Bunyan, Paul, 16-15
Buonarroti, Michelangelo, 6-22
butter, 12-24
buttercup, 9-17
butterfly, 1-9, 11-10, 11-24, 11-25,
    11-26
butterwort, 9-30
buttons, 15-26

C

CN Tower, 24-27
cacao bean, 12-23, 13-29
cactus, 9-8, 9-9
caffeine, 12-29
calculator, 22-8
camel, 14-18, 27-13
        roast, 12-31
camera, 22-12
canary, 19-9
candle, birthday cake, 8-5
candy, bestselling, 12-8
cane sugar, 12-27
canning food, 27-7
capillary, 2-24
Captain Hook, 26-8
Captain Nemo, 26-28
car, 6-31
        fastest, 4-9
carat, **18-28**
carbon dioxide, 9-10, 9-25, 19-16
        in pop, 12-22
carnivorous plants, 9-30, 9-31
Carolina wren, 7-26
carp, 5-26
Carroll, Lewis, 26-14, 26-21
carrot, 27-18
Carter, Howard, 6-5
cartilage, 19-30
cartoon, 10-10
Caspian Sea, 24-23
cassette player, miniature, 13-21
cat, 1-10, 1-14, 14-12
"cat out of the bag," 25-23

catacomb, **24-28**
caterpillar, 11-19, 11-26
catfish, 5-26
catgut, 10-21
Catherine the Great, 6-15
cell, 2-19, 2-23
centaur, 16-29
centipede, 1-8
centrifugal force, **22-16**
Ceres, 3-16
Challenger Deep, 3-24
chameleon, 17-29
        color of, 17-20
        diet of, 17-21
changeling, 26-12
Chapman, John, 6-24
Charles I, 26-21
Charles VI, 6-20
charley horse, 2-30
cheese, 12-24, 12-25, 14-20
cheetah, 1-17, 14-28
Cheshire Cat, 26-14
chess, 4-21
chewing gum, 13-11
chicken, 7-19, 7-24, 7-30
        beak of, 7-28
chicken pox, 19-22
children's literature, 10-24
Chimaera, 16-11
Chinese, 25-9
        ideograms, 25-17
        New Year, 8-18
        writing of, 13-16

chinook, 20-8, 20-9
Chiron, 16-29
chivalry, 15-24
chlorophyll, **9-11**, 9-14
chocolate, 13-29
chocolate bar, 12-23
chopsticks, 8-26
Christmas
    cards, 13-17
    carol, 8-9
    stocking, 8-13
    tree, 8-12
Churchill, Frank E., 26-30
chyme, 19-12
Cinderella, 26-31
circus, 10-16
cirrus, 20-24
city, most populous, 24-11
clam, 5-12
Cleopatra, 21-20
cloud, 3-11, 3-14, 20-13, 20-24
cloud seeding, 20-9
clown, 10-29
coat of arms, 25-7
cobra, 17-7, 17-15
coccyx, **19-13**
cocoa, 13-29
coconut, 9-7
cocoon, 11-13
codling moth, 11-18
Cody, William Frederick, 6-11
Coffin, Levi, 21-15
coins, 15-12
cold-blooded, 17-5, **17-30**
Collodi, Carlo, 26-9
color, 18-17
    blue, 18-17

red, 15-16
Colossus of Rhodes, 27-24
comet, 23-19
comic strip, 10-30
common cold, 19-18
communication
    animal, 1-14
    bee, 1-22
    coyote, 1-21
    cricket, 1-15
    dog, 25-5
    gorilla, 1-14
    lion, 1-11
compact disc, 22-7
compass, magnetic, 22-11
computer, 2-29, 18-22, 18-23
    memory, 22-9
conductor, orchestra, 10-15
Confucius, 6-14
confetti, 8-6
    at weddings, 8-7
constellations, **3-12**
Cook, Captain James, 6-26
copper, 18-28
copperhead, 17-6
copra, 9-7
coral, 24-8
coral snake, 17-6
cormorant, 7-18
corn, 12-21
cornucopia, 27-27
Cortes, Hernán, 21-16
Cotopaxi, 24-29
cotton candy, 12-9
cottonmouth, 17-6
country, smallest, 24-10
cow, 14-19

coyote, 1-20, 1-21
crab, 1-30
    hermit, 5-10
Crazy Horse, 6-10
cream, 12-24, 12-25
cricket, 1-15, 20-27
cricket, most runs, 27-9
Crockett, Davy, 16-14
crocodile, 17-18, 17-19
"crocodile tears," 25-25
crocodilian, **17-18**
crow, 1-19

crown, 8-14
Crusaders, 21-6
crustacean, **5-10**
cuckoo, 7-23
cumulonimbus, 20-24
cumulus, 20-24
Cupid, 16-17
curds and whey, 12-24
curse, 8-24
curveball, 4-13
Custer, General George, 6-10
cyclone, 20-23

D

Darrow, Charles, 4-6
Darwin, Charles, 24-17
Dauphin Charles, 6-20
Davy Jones' locker, **27-29**
dead language, 25-21
Dead Sea, 24-23
Dead Sea Scrolls, 21-13
deadly nightshade, 9-29
deer, 14-19
Demeter, 16-6
Denmark, flag of, 21-29
Devil's Triangle, 24-5
diamond, 3-19
diaphragm, **2-31**
digestion, human, 2-6, 2-7, 19-12
dinosaur, 1-24, 1-28
discovery, **13-28**
Disney, Walt, 6-23, 26-30
diving, 4-30

dizziness, 2-27
dodo, 7-8
dog, 1-14, 14-12, 14-13
    breeds, 15-18
    communication, 25-5
doldrums, 20-17
doll, 4-29
dolphin, 14-11
doughnut, 12-22
dracos, 17-28
Dracula, 16-21
dragon, 16-24
dragonfly, 11-25
dream, 2-10. *See also* nightmare
drum, 10-14
duck, 7-24
dugong, 16-25
dust, 15-23

E

eagle, 7-13, 7-27
ear, human, 2-8, 2-26, 2-27, 18-6
Earhart, Amelia, 6-12
earth, 3-21, 3-22, 23-17
    age of, 27-5
    atmosphere of, 23-22
    center, 3-6
    crust, 3-6, 3-24, 3-26
    gravity, 3-17
    orbit of, 23-31
    origin of, 27-5
    spin of, 23-31
    spinning of, 23-28
    weight of, 3-5
    wobble of, 23-30
earthball, 4-25
earthquake, 3-26
earthworm, 1-26
Easter bunny, 26-27
Easter eggs, 8-6
Easter Island, 24-16
eating, 2-6, 2-7
echo, 18-6, 18-7
echolocation, 14-7
eclipse, solar, 23-18
Edison, Thomas, 13-5, 13-30
eel, 5-14
eggplant, 9-6, 9-7
eggs

    insect, 11-19
    thousand-year-old, 12-30
egret, 14-25
Eiffel Tower, 24-2
Einstein, Albert, 6-18
electric eel, 5-14
electricity, 18-9, 18-14
    static, 18-8
electron, 18-8, 18-19
element, 18-15, **18-18**, 18-19
elephant, 14-21
    ears, 14-26
    heart rate of, 19-9
    memory of, 14-27
    trunk, 14-26
English, number of words, 25-8
epidermis, **2-12**
equator, **3-8**, **20-15**
Eric the Red, 3-31
etiquette, 8-27, 15-24
exoskelton, **11-5**
eye. *See also* vision
    human, 2-20, 2-21, 19-22, 19-26
    insect, 11-5, 11-14
    pupil, 19-26
    retina, **2-20**
eyebrows, 19-26
eyelashes, 2-13

F

Fables of Bidpai, 26-15
fairy, 26-11, 26-12
fairyland, 26-10
fairytale, 26-5, 26-15, 26-31
fangs, 17-15
fastest
    animal, 14-28
    bicycle, 13-18
    car, 4-9
    fish, 5-16
    snake, 17-31
    sport, 27-8
fasting, 2-7
feather, 1-12, 1-19, 7-19, 7-25
feathery, 4-12
femur, 2-8
fern, 9-22, 9-23
ferris wheel, 22-28
fever, 2-25
fibrin, **19-8**
fiddlehead, 9-22
Fiddler's Green, 27-29
finch, 7-13
fine arts, **10-5**
firecrackers, 13-12
firefly, 11-16, 11-17
fireweed, 9-19
fish
    age of, 5-22
    breathing, 1-7
    fastest, 5-16
    flying, 1-6
    largest, 5-17

    number of, 5-21
    sleep of, 1-7
    smallest, 5-5
    sushi, 12-21
fishing, 4-30
flag, 21-29
flamingo, 7-12, 7-13
flea, 11-14
Fleming, Alexander, 13-7
flight
    airplane, 18-31, 22-14
    bird, 1-19, 7-20, 7-21
    hang gliding, 4-10
    history of, 6-12, 6-13
    hot-air balloon, 13-10
    insect, 11-25
    jet, 18-31, 20-17, 22-14
    parachute, 18-21
    rocket, 18-30, 23-20, 23-31
    satellite, 23-13, 23-21
    Voyager I, 23-27
flipper, 1-5
flood, 20-20
flowers, 9-17
    largest, 9-16
fly, 1-9, 11-14
fly-fishing, 4-30
Flying Dutchman, 16-23
flying fish, 1-6
flying saucer. *See* UFO
flying trapeze, 10-29
fog, 3-10, **3-11**
folktale, 26-31

food
additives, 12-29
frozen, 13-24
fool's gold, 18-29
Ford, Henry, 6-31
fork, 8-26
freckles, 2-21
free fall, 4-11
French Revolution, 25-26
Freon, 22-26
Friday the 13th, 8-25

Frisbee, 13-20
frog, 1-25, 17-8, 17-9, 17-23, 17-26,
17-27
flying, 17-8
singing, 17-9, 17-23
tree, 17-9
frost, 18-27
frostbite, 19-10
funambulist, 10-28
fungi, 9-11, 9-13, 9-14
funny bone, 2-8

G

Galahad, 16-26
Galapagos Islands, 24-17
gallium, 18-14
gargoyles, 27-26
Gates, Bill, 13-31
Genghis Khan, 6-16
Geppetto, 26-9
germ, 18-24
geyser, 3-18, 3-19
ghosts, 27-28
Giant Sequoia, 9-27
giantism, 19-5
gibbon, 14-19
Gila monster, 17-13
gills, 5-22
giraffe, 14-18
Giza, 16-30
gizard, 7-28
glacier, 3-30, 3-31, 21-24

glass, 18-10
gnu, 14-31
goat, 14-19
goblin, 26-18
gold, 18-28, 18-29, 21-5
goldfish, 1-7, 5-16, 5-24
golf balls, 4-12
Goliath beetle, 11-10
good luck. *See* luck
goose, 7-24
goose bumps, 2-15
gorilla, 1-14, 14-8
gossamer, 11-30
Grand Canyon, 3-7
grass, 9-27
gravity, 3-17, 3-22, **18-21**,
23-22
Great Barrier Reef, 24-8
Great Fire of London, 21-19

Great Wall of China, 21-30
grebe, 7-27
Greek myths, 16-6, 16-7, 16-11, 16-12,
    16-13, 16-16, 16-18, 16-19, 16-29,
    24-25, 27-20
greenhouse effect, 20-29
Greenland, 3-31, 24-31
gremlin, 26-22
griffin, 16-31

groundhog, 14-15
grouse, 7-19
growth, human, 2-23
Gulliver's Travels, 26-20
gunpowder, 13-12
guppy, 5-16
Gutenberg, Johann, 6-6
Gutenberg Bible, 6-6

H

Hades, 16-6
haggis, 12-13
haiku, 10-12
hail, 20-9, 20-25
hair, human, 2-14, 2-15, 19-24, 19-25
Hallowe'en, 8-28
hamburger, 12-6
handshake, 8-21
hang gliding, 4-10
Hanging Gardens of Babylon, 27-24
Hannibal, 6-17
Hannukah, 8-8
"Happy Birthday to You," 15-9
Harlech Castle, 21-6
Harrison, George, 6-29
Hawaii, food of, 12-13
hawk, 7-5
hearing
    bird, 7-11
    human, 2-26, 18-6
    snake, 17-25, 17-31

heart, human, 19-9
heart rate, 19-9
Hector, 16-18
height, human, 2-23, 19-5, 19-30, 19-31
helium, 3-10, 18-20
hemoglobin, **19-7**, 19-17
Henry VII, 21-27
Henry VIII, 6-8
Hera, 16-18
Hercules, 16-18, 16-19
Hercules beetle, 11-10
heron, 7-19
herring, 5-27
hibernation, **14-7**
    amphibian, 17-5
hiccups, 2-31
Hickok, "Wild Bill," 6-11
high heels, 15-20
highest place in world, 24-21
hippopotamus, 14-25
hobgoblin, 26-13

hockey, 4-7
"holes in the head," 25-19
homing pigeon, 7-15
honey, 12-27
honeybee, 11-8, 11-9, 11-24
horn, **14-19**
horse, 11-15
    racing, 4-20, 14-29
horse latitudes, 20-15
hot dog, 12-6
Houdini, Harry, 10-22
housc sparrow, 7-19, 7-26
house wren, 7-26
housefly, 11-15
Hovercraft, 13-30
human being
    aging, 2-22
    baldness, 19-24
    belly button, 2-5
    blood, 2-24, 19-7, 19-8, 19-16,
        19-17
        circulation, 19-10
    blushing, 2-24
    bone, 2-8, 2-9, 19-7, 19-21
    brain, 2-16, 2-20, 2-22, 2-28, 2-29,
        2-31, 19-27
    breathing, 19-16
    coccyx, **19-13**
    diaphragm, **2-31**
    digestion, 2-6, 2-7, 19-12
    ear, 2-8, 2-26, 2-27, 18-6
    eye, 2-20, 2-21, 19-22, 19-26
    eyebrows, 19-26
    eyelashes, 2-13
    funny bone, 2-8
    hair, 2-14, 2-15, 19-24, 19-25
    hearing, 2-26, 18-6
    heart, 19-9
    height, 2-23, 19-5, 19-30, 19-31
    intestine, 2-6, 19-12
    lifespan, 2-22
    lung, 19-16, 19-17
    nervous system, 19-11
    pinkie finger, 19-19
    skeleton, 2-9
    skin, 2-12, 2-13, 2-25, 19-30
        color of, 19-12
        itching, 19-22
    sleep, 2-10, 2-11, 19-27
    tail, 19-13
    taste, 2-18
    teeth, 2-19, 19-6
    temperature, 19-28
    thumb, 19-19
    tongue, 2-18
    tonsils, 2-18
    vision, 2-20
        night blindness, 27-18
        snow blindness, 20-18
humidity, 20-26, 20-30
hummingbird, 1-18, 1-26, 7-13, 7-20
    bee, 7-27
humpback whale, 14-10
Humpty Dumpty, 26-21
Hundred Guineas Cup, 4-14
Hundred Years' War, 6-20, 21-28
hunger, 2-6
Huns, 27-23
hurricane, 20-9, 20-16, 20-23
Hydra, 16-18
hydrogen, 18-19, 18-20
hyena, 1-29
hygrometer, 20-11, 20-26
hypnotism, 19-14

I

ice, 3-8, 3-30, 18-12
Ice Age, 21-24, 21-25
ice boat, 4-15
ice cream, 12-14, 12-15, 12-26
ice cream cone, 12-14
iceberg, 27-31
ideograms, **25-17**
iguana, 17-28, 17-29
immune system, 19-20
incandescent, **22-19**
infection, 2-25
ink
    invisible, 22-29
    octopus, 5-24
    squid, 5-18
insect, **11-5**, 11-6
    as food, 12-5, 12-12

biggest, 11-10
blood, 11-6
eggs, 11-19
eyes, 11-5
flight of, 11-25
in winter, 11-24
number of, 11-11
intestine, human, 2-6, 19-12
invention, **13-28**
inventors, 13-31
Io moth, 11-19
ion, negative, 20-30
Islam, 24-19
island, largest, 24-31
itching, 19-22
ivy, English, 9-19

J

Jack Frost, 8-20, 18-27
Jack Pine Enduro, 4-19
jack-o'-lantern, 8-29
Jackson's chameleon, 17-29
jai alai, 27-8
Japan
    poetry (haiku), 10-12
    sushi, 12-21
    traditional home, 8-22
jazz, 10-27

Jefferson, Thomas, 6-30
jelly, 12-16
jellyfish, 5-15
jet flight, 18-31, 20-17, 22-14
jet stream, 20-16
jinx, 8-24
Joan of Arc, 6-20
joey, 14-22
joint, 2-9
juggling, 4-28

Julius Caesar, 21-20
jumping beans, 9-18
junk food, 12-28

Jupiter, 3-21, 23-26
    moons of, 23-15
    rings of, 23-27

K

Kalahari Desert, 24-7
kaleidoscope, 22-12
kangaroo, 11-14
    jumping, 14-23
    pouch, 14-22
Keller, Helen, 6-19
Kellogg, W.K., 27-6
kelp, 9-15
kettle, whistling, 15-31
kildeer, 7-26
King, Martin Luther, 6-19

King Arthur, 16-26, 16-27, 26-19
King Solomon, 6-14, 24-19
King Tut, 6-5, 21-11
kingfisher, 7-27
kite, 4-10
Klondike Gold Rush, 21-5
knight, 21-7, 26-19
"knock on wood," 8-23
knocker, 26-18
koala, 1-24
Krakatoa, 3-18

L

Labors of Hercules, 16-18
labyrinth, **27-10**
lacrosse, 4-21
Lake Baikal, 24-22
lake
    deepest, 24-22
    largest, 24-23
lake sturgeon, 5-27
lake trout, 5-26
Lancelot, 16-26

language. *See also* writing
    Chinese, 25-29
    dead, 25-21
    English, 25-8
    most common, 25-9
    number in the world, 25-8
    translation, 25-6
    variety of, 25-20, 25-21
    with most words, 25-8
lantern festival, 8-18

lantern fish, 5-19
Lapland, 24-30
largest
    bone, human, 2-8
    dish, 12-31
    fish, 5-17
    flower, 9-16
    insect, 11-10
    island, 24-31
    lake, 24-23
    planet, 23-26
    plant, 9-27
    rain forest, 24-24
    snake, 17-14
    town, 24-10
    volcano, active, 24-29
larva, 11-19
laser, 25-17
latitude, lines of, **20-15**
lava, 3-18
Lawrence of Arabia, 6-24
Lawrence, Thomas Edward, 6-24
leaf beetle, 11-24
Leaning Tower of Pisa, 24-27
leap year, 15-8
leaves, 9-20
left-handedness, 2-31
legend, **16-5**
lemming, 14-30
Lennon, John, 6-29
lens, camera, 22-12
Léotard, Jules, 10-29
leprechaun, 26-24
Lewis, C.S., 26-29
lichen, 19-14
licorice, 12-9
Life Savers, 12-8

lifespan, human, 2-22
ligaments, 2-9
light, **15-5**, 18-11, 18-17
    and plants, 9-11, 9-20, 9-24
    speed of, 3-14
lightbulb, 22-19
lighthouse, 22-18
lightning, 3-14, 20-6, 20-7
lightning rod, 20-6
Lilliput, 26-21
lily trotter, 7-16
limerick, **10-25**
Lincoln, Abraham, 6-30
Lindbergh, Charles, 6-13
Lindgren, Astrid, 26-23
lion, 1-11
"Little Jack Horner," 26-26
lizard, 17-20, 17-28, 17-29
lobster, 5-10
Loch Ness Monster, 16-25
lock, 22-10
locomotives, 22-15
London Bridge, 21-31
Lone Eagle, 6-13
longest
    palindrome, 25-17
    place name, 25-19
    river, 24-15
    word, 25-14
loon, 7-31
Lost Boys, 26-8
Louis XIV, 27-22
luau, 12-13
luck
    breaking mirror, 8-25
    Friday the 13th, 8-25
    horseshoes, 8-30, 8-31

"knock on wood," 8-23
thirteen, 8-25
walking under a ladder, 8-30
lung

amphibian, 17-5
human, 19-16, 19-17
lung fish, 5-20

M

magic, performance, 10-23, 22-17
magician, 10-23
magnet, 18-14
magnifying glass, 18-10
mamba, 17-31
mammal, **14-5**
    number of species of, 14-31
mammoth, 21-25
manatee, 16-25
mangrove tree, 9-19
manners. *See also* etiquette
    table, 8-27
maple syrup, 12-27
Marc Antony, 21-21
Marceau, Marcel, 10-18
Marianas Trench, 3-24
Marie Antoinette, 25-26
marionettes, 10-19
Mars, 3-21, 23-16
    moons of, 23-15
Mars, god of war, 16-12
marshmallows, 27-19
matches, 13-13
Mausoleum of Halicarnassus, 27-25
Mayas, 21-17
    writing of, 13-16

McCartney, Paul, 6-29
Mecca, 24-19
medicine, 27-30
Medusa, 16-7, 16-11
melanin, 2-12, 2-21
memory
    aid, 8-30
    computer, 22-9
    of elephants, 14-27
mental telepathy, 2-28
Mercury, 3-21
mercury, 18-26
meringue, 12-26
Merlin, 16-26, 16-27
mermaid, 16-25
metal, 18-14, **18-15**, 18-28
meteor, 3-13
meteorite, 3-13
meteorologist, 20-14, 20-23
Mexican jacana, 7-16
Mexico City, 24-11
Michelangelo, 6-22
microscope, 22-21
microwaves, 22-31
Midas, 26-25
Middle Ages, 21-26

migration, 1-18
milk, 12-15, 12-24, 12-27
milk chocolate, 12-23
milkshake, 12-15
mime, **10-18**
Minerva, 16-12
Minotaur, 27-20
mirror, 15-7, 18-11, 18-16
    and luck, 8-25
    in kaleidoscope, 22-12
mite, 11-7
moat, 21-6
moccasin, 17-15
Model T, 6-31
molecule, 18-12, 18-13, 18-14, **18-19**
monarch butterfly, 11-24
money, 15-28
monkey, 14-8
Monopoly, 4-6
monsoon, 20-14
moon
    atmosphere of, 23-12
    blue, 8-16
    full, 8-17
    gravity of, 3-17, 23-12
    orbit of, 23-15
    phases of, 23-23

    position of, 3-21
    size of, 23-14
moon dog, 23-25
moon landing, 6-30
moon vehicles, 23-10
moose, 14-19
mosquito, 1-29, 11-25
    bites, 11-28
moss, 9-12
moth, 1-9, 11-10, 11-19, 11-26
Mother Goose, 26-15
Mother's Day, 8-11
motorcycle, 4-19
Mount Everest, 24-21
Mount Isa, 24-10
Mount Kilimanjaro, 3-8
Mount Rushmore, 6-30
mouse, 14-20, 14-21
movies, 22-13
Mozart, Wolfgang Amadeus, 6-28
Muhammad, 24-19
mummy, 21-11
muscle, 2-30
mushroom, 9-13
muskellunge, 5-26
mussel, 5-13
myth, **16-6**

N

nacre, **5-12**
Napoleon, 21-23
Narnia, 26-29
Nashnush, Suleinan Ali, 4-9
Nautilus, 26-28
necktie, 15-11
neon, 22-19
Neptune, 3-21
    moons of, 23-15
Neptune, god of the sea, 16-13
Nero, 25-27
    "fiddled while Rome burned,"
      25-27
nerves, 2-14, 2-16, 2-17, 2-20, 2-24,
    2-26, 2-31
nervous system
    human, 19-11
Netherlands, 24-20
nettles, 9-28
Never-Never Land, 26-8
New Year's Eve, 8-19

newt, 17-16
nickel, 18-28
night blindness, 27-18
nighthawk, 7-17
Nightingale, Florence, 6-25
nightmare, 8-17
Nile, 24-15
nimbus, 20-24
Norse myths, 16-22
North Pole, 3-23, 3-25, 3-30
    magnetism of, 18-15
    northern lights, 23-19
    orientation to sun, 24-31
    weather of, 20-12
northern lights, 23-19
northern pike, 5-26
nova, 23-9
nucleus, **18-19**
nursery rhyme, 26-15
nuthatch, 7-17

O

Oakley, Annie, 27-15
    Wild West Show, 6-11
oarfish, 5-29
Oberon, 26-11
ocean, 3-5, 3-24, 3-25

octopus, 5-24, 5-25
Odin, 16-22
Oedipus, 16-30
Omohundro, "Texas Jack," 6-11
onion, 12-10

opera, 10-9
opossum, 14-14
orbit, **23-31**
orchestra, conductor, 10-15
osmosis, **18-13**
ostrich, 1-19, 1-26, 7-7, 7-22, 7-24
owl, 7-11, 7-30

oxpecker, 14-25
oxygen
    in human metabolism, 19-16,
      19-17
    in plant metabolism, 9-10, 9-25
oyster, 5-12

P

pacemaker, 22-31
Pacific Ocean, 20-13
pagoda, 24-12
pain, 2-14, 2-17
paint, 10-7
palindrome, **25-16**, 25-17
Pandora, 16-16
pantomime, 10-18
papyrus, 13-16
parachute, 18-21
Parker Brothers, 4-6
Parr, Catherine, 6-8
parrot, 7-7, 7-10
parrotfish, 5-23
Pasteur, Louis, 18-24
pasteurization, 12-24, 18-24
Pavlov, Ivan, 19-22
peacock, 1-12
peanut butter, 12-17
pearl, 5-12
pectin, 12-16
Pegasus, 16-11
pelican, 7-29

pencil, 15-29
pencil eraser, 22-28
penguin, 1-19, 7-7
    emperor, 7-26
penicillin, 13-7
perch, 5-20
percussion instrument, 10-14
perfume, 13-14
periscope, 18-16, 18-17
Perrault, Charles, 26-15
Persephone, 16-6
Perseus, 16-7
perspiration, 19-23
Peter III, 6-15
Peter Pan, 26-8
Peter Pan and Wendy, 26-8
Pharos of Alexandria, 27-25
phloem, **9-20**
phoenix, 16-31
photocopier, 22-9
photography, 22-12
photosynthesis, **9-11**
piano, 10-20

pickle, 12-18
pictogram, **25-17**
Pied Piper of Hamelin, 26-16
pigment, 19-12
    hair color, 19-25
pilchard, 5-27
pinkie finger, 19-19
Pinocchio, 26-9
Pippi Longstocking, 26-23
piranha, 5-7
pirate, 21-29
pitching, 4-13
pituitary gland, 19-5
pizza, 12-7
place name, longest, 25-19
planet, 3-16, 3-21
    largest, 23-26
    rings of, 23-27
    smallest, 23-26
plankton, 5-28
plant
    as medicine, 27-30
    breathing, 9-25
    color of, 9-11
    largest, 9-27
    number of species of, 9-5
    products of, 9-10
    reproduction of, 9-26
    sensitive, 9-23
    sleeping, 9-24
plantain, 12-16
platelet, **19-8**
Plato, 16-22
platypus, 14-22, 14-23
player piano, 10-20
playing cards, 4-27
Plimpton, James, 4-16

Pluto, 3-21, 23-26
Pocahontas, 27-14
poi, 12-13
poison
    frog, 17-9
    Gila monster, 17-13
    sea snake, 17-24
    snake, 17-6, 17-7
    toad, 17-22
poison ivy, 9-28, 19-22
pollen, **9-17**, 9-26
polliwog, 17-26
pollution, 20-28
polo, 4-25
Polyphemus moth, 11-11
Pompeii, 21-12
pop, 12-22
popcorn, 12-21
pope's ring, 8-15
popsicle, 13-24
porcupine, 14-15
Poseidon, 16-12, 16-13
Post, C.W., 27-6
potato, 9-29, 12-11
potato chips, 13-6
praying mantis, 11-27
precipitation, **20-14**
printing press, 6-6
Prince Vlad, 16-21
prospecting, 21-5
proton, **18-19**
proverb, **25-11**
public baths, 15-6
puck, hockey, 4-7
pulse, 19-9
Punch and Judy, 10-31
pupa, 11-26

pupil, 19-26
puppets, 10-19
purring, 1-10
Pygmy, 27-16, 27-17

pygmy goby, 5-5
Pyramids of Egypt, 21-10, 27-24
pyrite, 18-29
python, 17-14

Q

Queen Mab, 26-11
quicksand, 3-27

quill, porcupine, 14-15

R

rabbit, 1-14
raccoon, 14-30
racing
    auto, 4-9
    bicycle, 4-19
    motorcycle, 4-19
    sailboat, 4-14
radar, 20-11, 20-26
    acronym, 25-17
radio transmission, 22-6
radiosondes, 20-11
rafflesia, 9-16
Raggedy Ann doll, 13-28
rain, 3-28, 3-29, 20-9, 20-13, 20-20,
    20-23, 20-25, 20-31
    greatest rainfall, 20-21
    least rainfall, 20-21

rain dance, 20-31
rain forest, largest, 24-24
rainbow, 3-29, 20-25
rattlesnake, 17-6, 17-15, 17-25
rawinsondes, 20-11
"real McCoy," 25-18
rebus, **25-6**
red, 15-16
Red Baron, 6-12
red giant, 23-9
"red herring," 25-13
referee, 4-8
reflection, 18-11
reflex, **2-31**, 19-22
refrigeration, 22-26
reindeer, 24-30
relativity, 6-18

Renaissance, 6-22, 21-27
reptile, **17-5**
resonator, **18-6**
retina, **2-20**
returning top, 4-26
rhinoceros, 14-24, 16-29
rhinoceros beetle, 11-10
rice, 12-20, 12-21
Richthofen Circus, 6-12
ricksha, 24-13
right-handedness, 2-31
ring, 8-15
river, longest, 24-15
roadrunner, 1-20
roaring, 1-11

robin, 1-27
Robin Hood, 16-8
rocket, 18-30, 23-20
    orbit of, **23-31**
Roentgen, Wilhelm Konrad, 18-5
roller coaster, 22-16
roller skates, 4-16
Roman myths, 16-12, 16-16, 16-17
Romeo and Juliet, 6-7
Roosevelt, Theodore, 4-26, 6-30
rooster, 7-30
roots, 9-19
Rosetta Stone, 21-22
rubber, 4-7, 4-22

S

saga, **27-10**
saguarocactus, 9-8
Sahara, 3-9, 24-14
sailfish, 5-16
sailing, 4-14, 4-15
St. Elmo's fire, 20-7
St. Nicholas, 8-13
St. Peter's Basilica, 24-10
St. Stephen's Day, 8-13
salamander, 17-16, 17-17
salary, 25-28
saliva, 19-12
salmon, 5-30, 5-31
salt, 3-5, 12-18, 12-19, 18-12
"salt of the earth," 25-28

San, 24-7
sand, 27-12
sand martin, 7-27
sandwich, 12-7
sap, 12-27
sardine, 5-27
Sasquatch, 16-28
satellite, 23-13, 23-21
Saturn, 3-21
    moons of, 23-15
    rings of, 23-27
scab, 19-8
scales, 17-11, 17-31
Scheherazade, 26-7
school of fish, 5-17

scorpion, 11-7
scuba, 25-17
sea anemone, 5-19, 5-29
sea cucumber, 5-18, 5-29
sea horse, 5-11
sea snake, 17-24
seaweed, 9-15
    in sushi, 12-21
secretary bird, 7-16
seeds, 9-17, 9-26
sensitive plant, 9-23
Serengeti National Park, 1-16
Seven Wonders of the World, 27-24
shadow, 15-5
Shakespeare, William, 6-7
shark, 5-6
    hammerhead, 5-7
    whale, 5-17
sheep, 14-19
shelduck, 7-27
shellfish, 5-10
shivering, 19-28, 19-29
shoe
    history of, 15-27
    polishing, 15-10
shower, 22-23
shrew, 14-5
silicon, 18-22
silk, 11-12, 11-13, 11-30, 11-31
silkworm, 11-13
silver, 18-28
Sinbad, 26-7
Sistine Chapel, 6-22, 10-6
Sitting Bull, 6-10
skate sailing, 4-15
skeleton, 2-9
skiing, 4-7

skijaks, 13-8
skin, human, 2-12, 2-13, 2-25, 19-30
    color of, 19-12
    itching, 19-22
skull, 2-9
skunk, 1-31
sky, 3-29
sky surfing, 4-10
skydiving, 4-11
sleep
    fish, 1-7
    human, 2-10, 2-11, 19-27
sloth, 14-28
smallest
    bone, human, 2-8
    country, 24-10
    fish, 5-5
    planet, 23-26
snake, 17-6, 17-7, 17-15
    fastest, 17-31
    hearing of, 17-25, 17-31
    largest, 17-14
    movement of, 17-31
    sense of taste of, 17-6
    skin of, 1-31, 17-30
    teeth of, 17-15
snake charmer, 17-31
snow, 20-19, 20-20
    blindness, 20-18
    number of words for, 25-20
snowmobile, 13-25
soap, 22-25
soccer, 4-24
soccer stadium, largest, 4-24
soda pop, 12-22
solar flares, **23-19**
solar system, 27-5

Solomon, 6-14, 24-19
sonic boom, 18-31
sound, 2-26, 18-6, 18-7, 18-31
    first recording of, 13-5
    speed of, 3-14
sound recording, 13-5
South Pole, 3-23, 3-25, 3-30
    orientation to sun, 24-31
    weather of, 20-12
space, **23-22**
    size, 23-6
    temperatures, 23-11
space junk, 23-13
space travel, food for, 12-5
spacesuits, 23-11
spawning, 5-30
sperm whale, 5-9
Sphinx, 16-30
spicy food, 12-19
spider, 11-6, 11-7, 11-12, 11-21, 11-30
    11-31
spin, planetary, **23-31**
Spirit of St. Louis, 6-13
spitting cobra, 17-7
sponge, 5-23
sport
    fastest, 27-8
    slowest, 27-8
Sputnik 1, 23-21
squid
    giant, 5-8, 5-29
    ink, 5-18
stairs, creaky, 15-21
stalactites, **3-7**
stalagmites, **3-7**
star, 3-11, 3-12
    color of, 23-6

distance from earth of, 23-7
number of, 23-5
size of, 23-9
speed of, 23-7
starfish, 5-11, 5-18
starling, 7-26
Starr, Ringo, 6-29
Statue of Zeus at Olympia, 27-25
steel, stainless, 18-15
steeplechase, 4-20
Stoker, Bram, 16-21
stomach, human, 2-6, 2-31
stop sign, 15-16
''straight from the horse's mouth,''
    25-22
stratus, 20-24
Strauss, Levi, 13-26
Stuart, Charles Edward, 6-9
Styx, 16-18, 25-24
submarine, 18-16, 18-17
    invention of, 13-9
sugar, 12-27
Sullivan, Anne, 6-19
Sumerians, writing of, 13-16
sun dog, 23-25
sun, 3-11, 3-16, 3-21, 3-29, 18-17
    distance from earth, 23-24
    size of, 23-9
    solar flares, **23-19**
    temperature of, 23-24
sundews, 9-31
sunspots, 23-25
sunstroke, 19-15
supernova, 23-9
surf board, 4-5
surfing, 4-5
surname, 8-21

sushi, 12-21
swan, 7-21, 7-24
sweat, 2-24

Swift, Jonathan, 26-20
Swiss cheese, 12-23
symbiosis, **9-14**

T

tadpole, 1-25, 17-26, 17-27
tail, human, 19-13
tailorbird, 7-8
Taj Mahal, 24-6
tallest animal, 14-18
tandem bicycle, 4-18
tarantula, 11-21
target, 4-31
Tarot cards, 4-27
taste, human, 2-18
Tchaikovsky, 1812 Overture, 10-15
tea, 25-30
tears, 2-20
teddy bear, 4-27
teeth
    human, 2-19, 19-6
    snake, 17-15
telescope, 22-20, 22-21
temperature, 18-26
    measurement of, 20-26, 20-27
    of the human body, 19-28
Temple of Artemis, 27-25
Temujin, 6-16
thermometer, 18-26, 20-26
thermos bottle, 15-31
Theseus, 27-20
thigh bone. *See* femur

thirst, 19-23
thirteen, unlucky, 8-25
thread snake, 17-15
Three Little Pigs, 26-30
Three Wishes, The, 26-6
thumb, human, 19-19
thunder, 3-14
thunderstorm, 20-7
tick, 11-7
tickling, 2-17
tides, 3-24, 3-25
tightrope walking, 10-28
Timbuktu, 24-11
Titan, 16-19
Titania, 26-11
Titanic, 21-18
toad, 1-25, 17-22, 17-23, 17-26
toaster, 22-27
toilet, 22-23
Tokyo, 24-11
tomato, 9-29
tongue
    chameleon, 17-21
    human, 2-18
    snake, 17-6
tonsils, 2-18
tooth fairy, 26-10

toothbrush, 13-22
toothpaste tube, 22-24
toothpicks, 15-22
tornado, 3-15, 3-28, 20-16
totem pole, 21-9
town, largest, 24-10
translation, 25-6
tree, 9-5, 9-20, 9-21
trident, 16-13
triggerfish, 1-7
triskaidekaphobia, **8-25**
Trojan War, 16-18, 25-24

troposphere, **20-5**
truffle, 12-11
tuatara, 17-12
Tubman, Harriet, 21-15
tundra, 3-9
turkey, 7-24
turtle, 17-10, 17-11
Tutankhamen, 6-5, 21-11
tutu, 10-8
Twenty Thousand Leagues Under the Sea, 26-28
typhoon, 20-23

U

UFO, 3-20
umbrella, 15-14
Underground Railroad, 21-14
unicorn, 16-10, 16-29
unicycle, 4-18

Uranus, 3-21
    moons of, 23-15
    rings of, 23-27
Ursa Major, 3-12

V

vaccine, 18-24
vacuum, **15-31**
Valentine's Day, 8-10
Valhalla, 16-22
Valley of Kings, 6-5, 21-10
vampire, 16-21
Van Winkle, Rip, 16-14

Vatican, 24-10
Velcro, 13-14
vending machine, 22-5
venom, 17-6, 17-7, 17-15
Venus, 3-21
Venus, goddess of love, 16-12, 16-16, 16-17

Verne, Jules, 26-28
vertebrate, **5-5**
Vespucci, Amerigo, 21-15
Vesta, 3-16
Vesuvius, 21-12
Viking, 21-14
vinegar, 12-18
violin, strings, 10-21
viper, 17-15
virus, 19-18, 19-20
vision. *See also* eye
 color, 14-25

human, 2-20
 night blindness, 27-18
 snow blindness, 20-18
Vitamin A, 27-18
volcano, 3-18, 3-19
 largest active, 24-29
 Vesuvius, 21-12
volume, measurement of, 18-28
von Richthofen, Baron Manfred, 6-12
Voyager I, 23-27
Vulcan, 16-16
vulcanization, **4-7**

W

waffle, 12-14
Wailing Wall, 24-19
walking, 2-13
walkingstick, 11-10
warm-blooded, 19-28
Wars of the Roses, 21-26
wart, 17-22, 19-20
Washington, George, 6-30
wasp, 11-28
water, 3-22, 18-12, 18-13, 18-18, 18-19,
 20-13
 city systems of, 15-15
 color of, 18-17
water pressure, 22-22
waterfall, 3-23
waterspout, 20-22
waves, 3-22
weather, 20-5

and mood, 20-30
 control of, 20-9
 prediction of, 20-14, 20-26
  by animals, 20-27
weather balloon, 20-11
weather vane, 20-10, 20-26
web, spider, 11-12, 11-31
wedding ring, 8-15
weed, **9-25**
werewolf, 16-20
whale, 1-5, 14-5, 14-10, 14-11
 blue, 1-24
 humpback, 14-10
 sperm, 5-9
whale shark, 5-17
wheel, 13-19
whey, 12-24
whippoorwill, 7-26

white dwarf, 23-9
"white elephant," 25-31
"Who's afraid of the Big Bad Wolf?"
    26-30
wicca, 16-20
Wild West Show, 6-11
willy-willies, 20-23
wind, 3-15, 20-9, 20-16, 20-17
    and mood, 20-23
    monsoon, 20-14
windshield wipers, 15-17
wings, 1-19
winking, 2-21
wishes, 26-6

witch, 16-20
wolf, 14-13
woodpecker, 1-13
word
    longest, 25-14
    with most meanings, 25-11
wrinkles, 19-30
writing
    ancient Egyptian, 13-16
    Chinese, 13-16
    ideograms, **25-17**
    invention of, 13-16
    Mayan, 13-16
    Sumerian, 13-16

XYZ

X-ray, 18-5
yak, 14-19
yawn, 19-27
yo-yo, 4-26
zebra, 14-24

zeppelin, 18-20
Zeus, 16-12, 16-13, 16-18
zinc, 18-28
zipper, 13-27
zoologist, **18-25**